What Is a Plant?

HOUGHTON MIFFLIN HARCOURT

PHOTOGRAPHY CREDITS: (c) ©Corbis; 3 (b) © Tony Fagan/Alamy; 4 (t) ©luca gargano/Flickr Open/Getty Images; 4 (b) Michael P Gadomski/Getty Images; 6 (b) ©Comstock Images/Jupiterimages/Getty Images; 8 (t) ©Tony Hertz/ AgStock Images/Corbis; 9 (b) ©Ross M Horowitz/Stone/Getty Images; 10 (bl) ©Richard Griffin/Alamy Images; 11 (tl) AgStock Images/Corbis; 11 (tr) ©Todd Muskopf/Alamy Images

Printed in Mexico

ISBN: 978-0-544-07217-6

3 4 5 6 7 8 9 10 0908 21 20 19 18 17 16 15 14

4500469985   A B C D E F G

Be an Active Reader!

Look for each word in yellow along with its meaning.

seed	stem	flower	cone
root	leaf	fruit	

Underlined sentences answer the questions.

How are plants different from animals?

What are seeds and roots?

What plant parts can we see?

How does a plant use its parts?

How are flowers different from cones?

How are young plants and their parents alike and different?

What are some ways we sort plants?

How are plants different from animals?

Animals can not make their own food. They eat plants or other animals. Plants can make their own food. Plants can not move like animals.

Rabbits hop. Plants do not hop.

What are seeds and roots?

A covering protects a seed.

A tiny plant begins inside a seed.

Many new plants grow from seeds. A seed is the part of a plant that new plants grow from.

Seeds grow in soil.

Plants have roots. A root grows down into the soil. Roots hold the plant in place. Roots take in water and nutrients from the soil. Nutrients are things in soil that help plants grow.

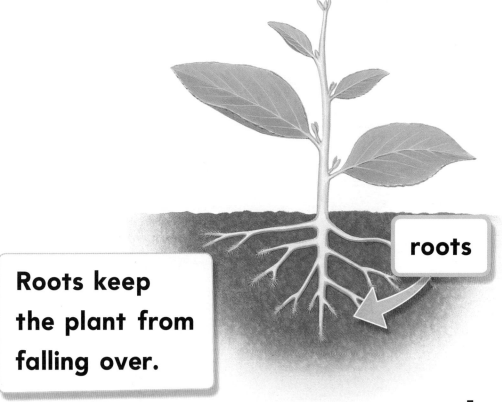

roots

Roots keep the plant from falling over.

What plant parts can we see?

A stem holds the plant up. Stems move water and nutrients to all plant parts. A leaf makes food for the plant. It uses light, air, and water. A flower is the part that makes seeds.

flower

leaf

stem

How does a plant use its parts?

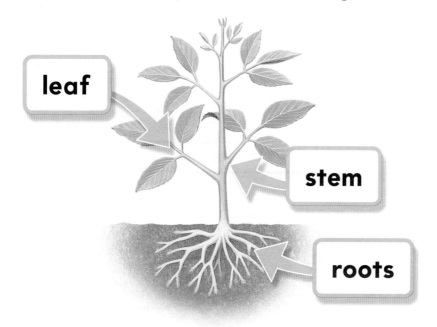

The plant uses its parts to make food.
Roots carry water and nutrients to
the stem. The stem carries water and
nutrients to the leaves. Leaves make
food for the plant.

How are flowers different from cones?

An orange tree has flowers.

Some plants have parts that other plants do not. Some trees have flowers. Fruit trees grow flowers. Deep inside the flower are parts that can form fruit. A fruit is the part of the plant that holds seeds.

Some trees have cones. The cone is a part of a non-flowering plant. The cone holds seeds. Cones open. Seeds fall to the ground. New trees can grow.

A pine tree has cones.

How are young plants and their parents alike and different?

Young plants can have a leaf shape much like their parents'. Young plants are smaller. They do not have flowers or fruits.

young tomato plant

adult tomato plant

We can eat fruit from an apple tree.

These leaves were green.

What are some ways we sort plants?

There are plants we can eat. We can eat apples from an apple tree. Some other plants we cannot eat. Some trees stay green all year round. Other trees turn different colors.

Be a Scientist

Work with a partner. Go outside. Look at the different parts of plants. Use a hand lens. Ask yourself questions: Do I see seeds, roots, and stems? Does this plant have flowers or cones? Are the leaves big or small?

 ## Write About Plants

Cut out magazine pictures of different kinds of plants. Glue each picture on an index card. Label the parts. Show a friend each picture. Invite him or her to tell about it.